THE WORLD AROUND US!
SEEING

Jillian Phillips

Dover Publications, Inc.
Mineola, New York

Copyright

Bibliographical Note

The World Around Us! Seeing is a new work, first published by Dover Publications, Inc., in 2010.

International Standard Book Number
ISBN-13: 978-0-486-47731-2
ISBN-10: 0-486-47731-2

Manufactured in the United States by Courier Corporation
47731201
www.doverpublications.com

You have 2 **EYES** to see things.

Look who's at the pond!

bread

How many MonkeyS can you SEE in the tree?

Write down 10 things you can see out of your window.

1 ....

2 ....

3 ....

4 ....

5 ....

6 ....

7 ....

8 ....

9 ....

10 ....

EYES information

info

From the moment you wake up in the morning to when you go to bed at night, your **EYES** are taking pictures of the world around you. They send these pictures to your **BRAIN** and your brain works out what you are seeing.

Your eye works like a **Camera**.
Light passes through the **lens** in your eye, and your **RETINA**, at the back of your eye, records it.

Your eye actually takes pictures upside down, but when the **BRAIN** receives it, it flips it the right way up so you know what you are seeing!

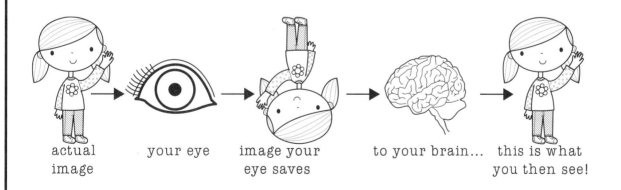

actual image   your eye   image your eye saves   to your brain...   this is what you then see!

LET'S HAVE A CLOSER LOOK!.......

5

LOOK *Inside your Eye*

info

What are the parts of your eye and what do they do?

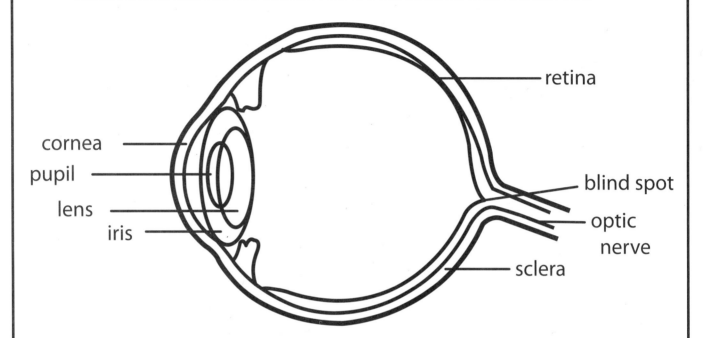

cornea
pupil
lens
iris

retina
blind spot
optic nerve
sclera

Cornea: This is the see-through skin that covers your eye.

Sclera: This is skin that covers the outside of the eyeball, also known as the "white" of the eye.

Iris: The iris is the colored part of your eye that controls the amount of light that enters the eye.

Pupil: This is the hole in the iris that lets light through. When it is in bright light it gets very small. When it is in the dark, it gets bigger.

Lens: The lens focuses light on to the retina. It changes shape when it's focusing so that the picture is as clear as possible.

Retina: This acts as a screen to show the pictures you are seeing. It turns the picture into an electrical message, which it then sends to your brain.

Blind Spot: This is part of the retina, but it's not sensitive to light. It's also the spot where the retina is joined to the optic nerve.

Optic Nerve: The electrical messages from the retina travel along here to the brain.

what can you see in the
GARDEN?

EYES ARE AMAZING!

Eyes help us see all sorts of things:

PEOPLE

TV

Nature

Animals

Colors

CLOUDS

red

yellow

blue

What other things can you see?

....

....

....

....

What's your **FAVORITE** thing that you can see?

....

At the end of the day your
eyes need to rest. It's time for bed.

During the **day** the Sun gives
us natural light, and it's easy
to see things.

At nighttime it is
hard to see
anything in the dark—

so you have to switch on a light!

PUPILS: LOOK CLOSER!

The **IRIS** controls how much light is let into your eye.
Look at your eyes in a mirror.
Can you see the black **PUPIL** in the center?
Look at its size.

Now, cup your hand around your eye so it is shaded from any light and see what happens to the size of the pupil.
It gets bigger!

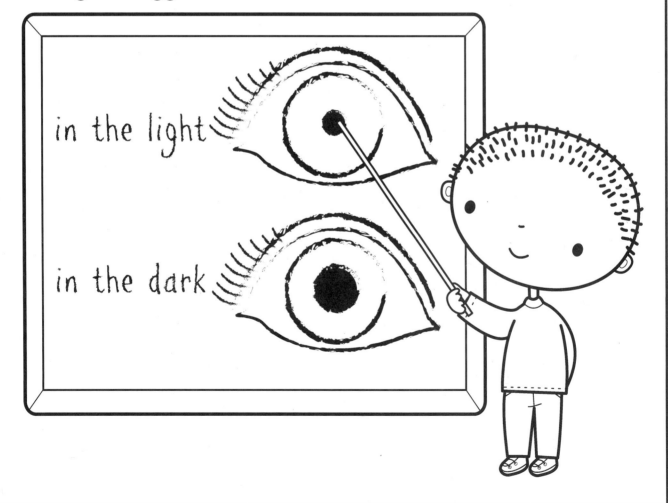

in the light

in the dark

LOOK *at some Animal eyes*

OWLS have **big** eyes

MOLES have really small eyes

ANIMAL Eye Facts

CATS have excellent night vision.

Dogs can't see in color but they have a wide field of vision.

A **Fly** has eyes that help it see in all directions at once and are very good at detecting motion.

FROGS have round bulging eyes that help them see almost all the way around themselves without moving their heads.

FISH have no tear ducts or eyelids. They sleep with their eyes open!

Owls have very good night vision and see mainly in black and white.

Write down the different animals you can see at the Zoo...

Reptile House

ZOO

Binoculars help you see things that are **FAR AWAY.**

Each of your eyes sees
slightly different pictures.
Your brain puts
the two images together
into a single picture.

Guide dogs help visually
impaired people get around.

Some people wear **glasses**
to **see** better.

The **OPTICIAN** tests your **EYES** to see if you need to wear glasses.

EYE Color

activity

Our eye color depends on how much pigment we have in our irises. Brown eyes have more pigment and blue eyes have less.

WHAT COLOR ARE YOUR EYES?

✓ check box ☐ brown ☐ blue ☐ green ☐ hazel ☐ _____

Now, find out what color eyes your family and friends have!

NAME	COLOR
. . . .	. . . .
. . . .	. . . .
. . . .	. . . .
. . . .	. . . .
. . . .	. . . .
. . . .	. . . .

TEARS: Why do you cry tears?

info

Whether you are awake, asleep, happy, or sad, tears are always flowing from your tear glands.

Tears flow from **TEAR GLANDS** into your eyes through tiny tear ducts. The tear glands are under your upper lids, and their job is to make tears to keep the surface of your eyeball clean and **MOIST**, and to help **PROTECT** your eye from damage.

Every time you blink, a fluid spreads over your eyes.

Tear glands produce more fluid when your eyes are irritated. Small things that are on your eye (like specks of dust) wash into the corner of your eye next to your nose.
Sometimes tears flow over your lower eyelid (when you cry, or you have allergies), but mostly the tears flow down a tiny tube at the edge of your lower eyelid, next to your nose.
(If you look very carefully you can see a tiny dot that is the beginning of that tube).
This tube carries the tears to the back of your nose (and this is why your nose "runs" when you cry!)

HAPPY   SAD

TAKE CARE OF YOUR EYES!

Your eyes need light to see, but there is a kind of light that is harmful to your eyes. This is called Ultra Violet light (or UV for short).
When it's very sunny, UV light is very strong, so you need to wear sunglasses!

Don't forget to wear them.

What do you see
at the **BEACH**?

What colors can you see?

....

....

....

Color in these Fruits!

Green **Red** **Yellow** **Orange**

COLOR IN THE SHAPES BELOW

BLUE   RED   ORANGE   PURPLE   BROWN

What's your favorite color?

• •

How many COLORS do you see in a rainbow?

How much can you SEE?

(1) **Can you see what is off to the side?**

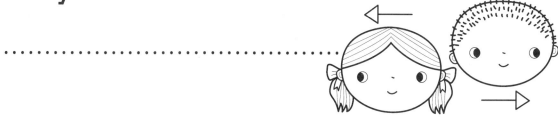

....

(2) **Put you arm out in front of you.
Can you focus on your hand and what
is in the distance at the same time?**

....

(3) **At nighttime, see how long it takes
you to see things in the dark when
the lights are switched off.**

....

What can you see now?